Photography - Christopher Upham

Design - MJ Connors Davison

Layout - Logan Veith

Copyright 2020

Prints available at www.christopherupham.com

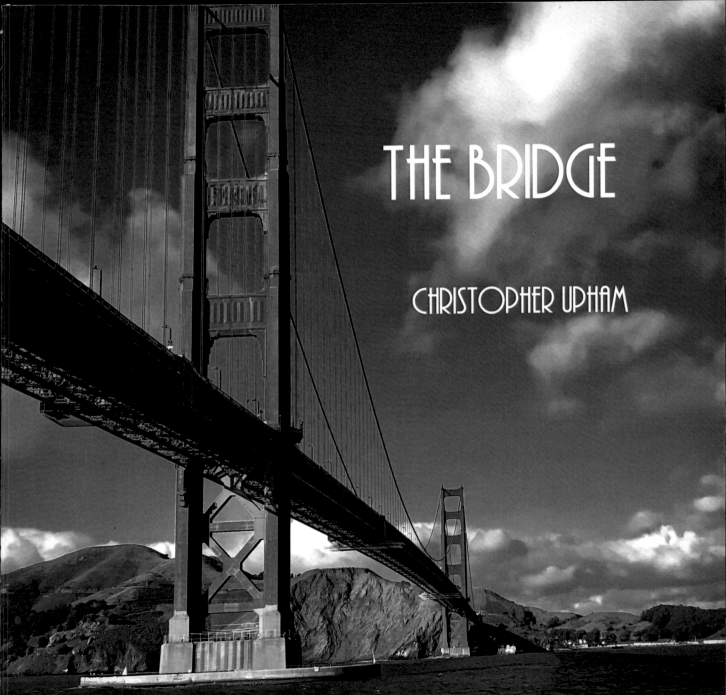

THE BRIDGE

CHRISTOPHER UPHAM

Christopher Upham is a writer, filmmaker, actor, and photographer living in San Francisco. He has bicycled across the Golden Gate Bridge more than six thousand times.

CEREUS

mjconnorsdavison.com
loredesignllc.com